# Contents

KU-612-546

(Note: words printed in **bold italics** are explained in the glossary.)

# Meet Nick

Do you like tinkering with machines? Nick does! For as long as he can remember he has enjoyed taking things apart to see how they work – and then putting them back together again. That's why he decided on a **career** with cars.

> **Nick started his apprenticeship at the garage about 18 months ago.** ▶

Nick left school at 16 and was taken on as an **apprentice** at his local garage. There are lots of different jobs in the motor industry, and apprenticeships for each, but Nick is training to be a mechanic. This means that he is based in the garage workshop, where cars are serviced.

# I work in a Garage

## by Clare Oliver

### Photography by Chris Fairclough

**W**

**FRANKLIN WATTS**
LONDON • SYDNEY

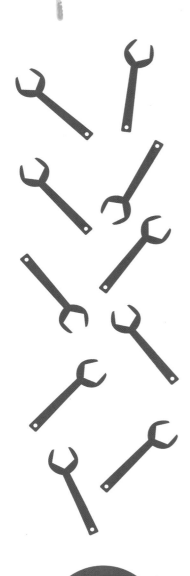

First published in 2001 by
Franklin Watts
96 Leonard Street
London
EC2A 4XD

Franklin Watts Australia
56 O'Riordan Street
Alexandria
NSW 2015

ISBN: 0 7496 4059 6
Dewey Decimal Classification 629.28
A CIP catalogue reference for this book is available
from the British Library

Printed in Malaysia

Editor: Kate Banham
Designer: Joelle Wheelwright
Art Direction: Jason Anscomb
Photography: Chris Fairclough
Consultant: Beverley Mathias, REACH
REACH is the National Advice Centre for Children with Reading
Difficulties. REACH can be contacted at California Country Park,
Nine Mile Ride, Finchampstead, Berkshire RG40 4HT. Check out
the website at **reach-reading@demon.co.uk** or email them at
**reach@reach-reading.demon.co.uk**.

Acknowledgements
The publishers would like to thank Nick Horn and the
staff of F.G. Barnes, Maidstone, Kent, for their help in
the production of this book.

**N**ick doesn't have to take exams. Instead, he is being trained on the job, by the workshop *foreman*, Bill. Nick can take things at his own pace, but at the end of his apprenticeship he will be a *qualified* mechanic. He is about halfway through now. He has already learned enough to do simple jobs by himself without Bill's help.

Bill is Nick's *mentor*. Nick can rely on him for help and training.

Nick can do routine jobs without any help. Here, he is tightening the hose clamp.

## Mechanic

JUST THE JOB!

Nick's regular tasks include:
- Identifying engine problems
- Fixing faulty engines and fitting new parts
- Servicing vehicles so that they are kept at their best
- Getting vehicles ready to return to the customer

# The Busy Garage

The company that Nick works for is involved in every aspect of the motor trade. Firstly, there is a car showroom with a large forecourt, where there are displays of new cars for sale. Sometimes, Nick has to move them around.

John, the general manager, takes a special interest in how all the apprentices are getting on. ▶

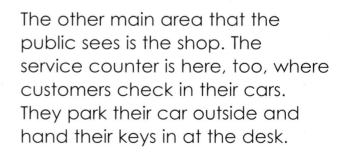

The other main area that the public sees is the shop. The service counter is here, too, where customers check in their cars. They park their car outside and hand their keys in at the desk.

◀ The parts shop sells items such as hub caps and engine oil.

## Favourite Five

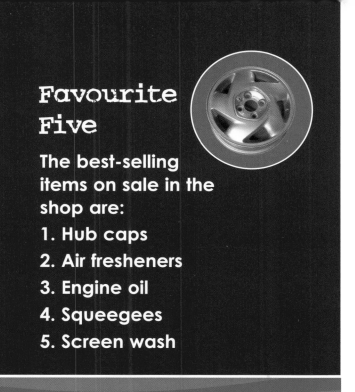

The best-selling items on sale in the shop are:
1. Hub caps
2. Air fresheners
3. Engine oil
4. Squeegees
5. Screen wash

Nick sometimes fetches exhausts or other parts from the warehouse.

Behind the scenes are the workshop, the bodyshop and the paintshop. Cars that are in for a service or normal mechanical repairs are fixed in the workshop. Cars that have been in an accident and are badly damaged need to be rebuilt in the bodyshop, and resprayed in the paintshop.

Customers' car keys are kept on numbered pegs. Before Nick can service a car, he has to drive it into the workshop.

The company also has lots of offices, and a warehouse where all the spare parts are stored. Upstairs, there are more offices and a **conference room**. These are for business customers to use while they are waiting for their car to be fixed.

# In for a Service

W hen customers want their car serviced, they ring the garage. Greg, John and John spend almost all day on the phone taking service bookings. They ask each customer for details about the car, including the *model* and registration number.

As they do this, they fill in a job card. This is slipped into a date and time slot on the wall. There are only so many slots per day, so the three sales managers don't book in more cars than the mechanics can handle.

The service sales managers take bookings by phone.

## Service Sales Manager

Greg, John and John are experienced at their job. They know just the right questions to ask on the phone. They need to *estimate* exactly how long a service will take, and how much it will cost the customer. If they make a mistake, the car could be late back to the customer, which would not be good for business.

JUST THE JOB!

10

> John slips a job card into a pocket on the wall. The pocket shows the date and time that the car will be serviced. ▶

**E**ach morning Dave, the workshop controller, collects the cards for all the cars that need servicing that day. Then he **allocates** the cards, deciding which mechanics will work on which cars.

> Dave gives Nick his job card. This tells Nick which car to work on and what needs doing to it. ▼

Tricky jobs usually go to the most experienced mechanics, but Dave knows that Nick is there to learn. Whenever Dave can, he gives Nick one of the more difficult jobs, or one that will teach him new skills. When this happens, Dave asks Bill, Nick's trainer, to show him how to do the job.

# The Workshop

The workshop is always busy, with mechanics driving cars in and out. Each mechanic has their own working area, or bay.

Nick felt really proud when he got his own bay. At the back of the bay is a workbench, where Nick keeps his tool box and fresh jugs of engine oil and water. Nick also has two or three clip-on lights. He can fix these so they shine right on the spot where he is working.

> **Nick carries a new car exhaust to his bay.**

## Jobspeak

You need to know the different parts of a car to be a mechanic. Here are some of the main ones:

*brake pad* – material in a disc brake that presses against the wheels to stop them turning

*carburettor* – the part of an engine where fuel and air mix and *ignite* to fire the cylinders

*choke valve* – the part that controls how much air enters the carburettor

*radiator* – the *grille* that lets heat from the engine escape into the air

*transmission* – the different parts that carry power to the wheels to make them move

On the workshop wall there is a set of *specialist* tools for everyone to share.

## Essential Kit

Nick's clothing and accessories protect his body and own clothes from damage:

- **Smart grey and red overalls**
- **Shoes strengthened with steel toe caps**
- **_Disposable_ vinyl gloves to keep oil off his hands**
- **Safety goggles to wear when _welding_**
- **Ear protectors to wear for noisy jobs**

The bay has a lifting device, so that Nick can work on the underside of a car without having to crawl underneath. There is also an exhaust-fume extractor. This is a pipe that fits to the car exhaust when Nick is checking a running engine. The pipe carries the fumes safely out of the workshop, so the mechanics don't breathe in dangerous gases.

Nick wears vinyl gloves to protect his hands from grease and oil.

13

# Spare Parts

When Nick services a car, he goes to the parts desk to get any items that he needs. All the parts are stored in the warehouse. Even if Nick needs only a single jug of oil, he must tell John, the Parts Manager. John enters what Nick has taken into the computer, along with what job the item was for. This means there is a perfect record of what is used for each service. It allows the company to keep track of things and charge the customer a fair price.

Nick fills a jug full of oil. This has to be signed out against a particular job.

## Tricky Moments

An important part of John's job is to order new parts. He has to keep enough parts in stock but not too many. New models of car appear each year, often requiring their own special parts, but many people drive older cars.

It would tie up too much of the company's money – and space – to keep a part to cover every emergency. John simply has to make an informed guess.

**A**ll of the different parts are delivered to the back entrance of the warehouse on *rollcages*. John, or one of his assistants, checks off the goods as they arrive and signs for the delivery. There are parts for many different *makes* and models of car.

This new car door is going to be fitted on to a red car. It will be spraypainted to match.

There is a wide selection of wrapped-up car bumpers on the top floor of the warehouse.

# The Bodyshop

Crumpled cars end up in the bodyshop, the part of the garage where cars' bodies, or **shells**, are fixed. Nick has had to do a tiny bit of training in this area, just so that he can get a more rounded picture of the motor industry.

Bodyshop worker Paul is using a special tool to smooth the inner shell of this car.

Nick is helping Mick, one of the bodyshop workers, to fix a fender.

The main job that goes on in the bodyshop is **panel beating**. This means knocking back into shape the metal sheets that make the shell of the vehicle. **Blowtorches** are a key piece of equipment in the bodyshop, because the bodywork needs to be heated to become **pliable**. Smaller dents are tapped out using a small pin hammer or chisel.

Before any work can happen to the body of a car that has been in an accident, the garage needs to record the damage. This is because accident repairs are usually paid for by an insurance company and they need to agree the work first.

Nowadays, this process does not take long. The garage films the damaged vehicle using a digital video camera, then e-mails the footage direct to the insurers. Usually, they get an 'OK' in a matter of minutes!

## Bodyshop Worker

The bodyshop workers' main duties are:

- **Repairing body panels**
- **Replacing body panels and panel sections**
- **Straightening out panels that are skewed (don't line up)**

Nick is filming this car for the insurance company. Hopefully, they will pay for the repairs.

# Perfect Paintwork

**C**ars that have been fitted with new panels or been scratched are resprayed in the paintshop.

Matching the paint colour is a skilled business. Every car has a code number, which tells the paintshop workers the exact shade of its original paint. They can look up the code in a reference *manual*, to discover how to mix the right colour. Sounds easy, doesn't it?

## Top Five

The paint colours that are mixed most often are:
1. White
2. Silver
3. Red
4. Blue
5. Black

John mixes some white paint. No one can stand the paint fumes in the mixing room for long.

However, the code only tells what colour the car was when it was brand-new. It doesn't allow for three years of fading in the sun, for example! Luckily the most experienced paintshop workers can adjust the colour to match exactly.

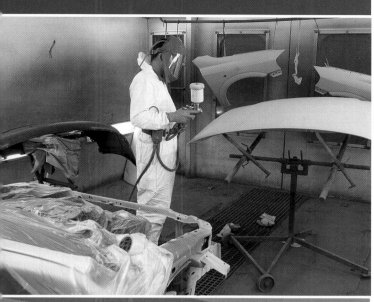

Spraypainting is done in a garage-sized oven. John moves his arm in steady, sweeping gestures to achieve a fine, even mist.

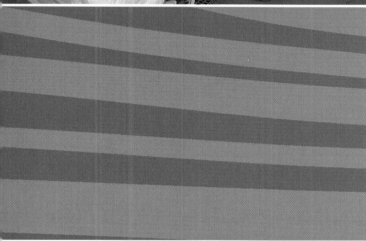

The spraypainting itself happens in a cool, dry 'oven'. The worker wears goggles and a face mask, as well as disposable white overalls. Once the vehicle has been evenly sprayed with paint, it is left to 'bake' for two to three hours. This allows the paint to harden. Finally, the car is **buffed**, waxed and polished, for a super-shiny finish.

Richard, the paintshop apprentice, uses a special polishing machine to buff this newly-painted car.

19

# Customer Care

Servicing, rebuilding or respraying a car is not the end of the story. All the cars need to be thoroughly cleaned before they are picked up by their owners. There is a special 'garage' that is just large enough for one car and has its own water and electricity supply. Here, a car can be hosed down and polished and the interior can be vacuumed.

Cars are hosed down in the cleaning garage.

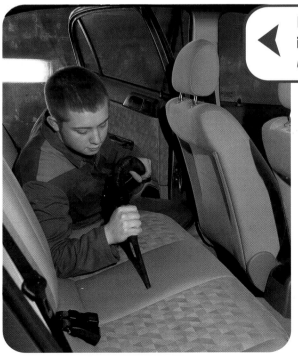

Nick spruces up the car's interior by vacuuming all the *upholstery* and carpets.

The company that Nick works for offers customers other services, too. Some people use the conference facilities and offices to get on with work while they are waiting for their car to be serviced. Other people have to leave and get back into town. For these people, the company provides a minibus.

ony drives the minibus, and he gives customers a lift home or to their office. The minibus is also used to pick up a few employees from the station in the morning and drop them off in the evening – although most of the staff have their own transport.

Nick helps Elaine, one of the office workers, out of Tony's minibus. Mostly, though, the bus is used for customers.

## Minibus Driver

*JUST THE JOB!*

Tony has worked as the company driver for more than ten years. Most of the time, he drives the minibus. However, he also takes *courtesy cars* out to some of the customers and picks up their car at the same time. This saves them the trouble of having to drive it to the garage themselves.

# Sales and Test-Drives

Usually, the company where Nick works has an apprentice working in the sales department. Sales is a very different kind of job to being a mechanic. You don't need to know so much about how things work, but you do need to be very good at talking to people.

Tammy and Lynne are two of the company's best sales executives.

A salesperson has to listen carefully to what a customer says, to find out exactly what kind of car they want to buy – and then sell it to them!

All of the sold cars go out to the customer with a company key fob. This is good advertising for the company.

No one knows how many customers will come in on a particular day, and the sales workers need to use any free time efficiently.

They find out more about the cars they are selling and estimate how many sales they expect to make in the coming year. They contact companies that might hire or buy company cars. They also read motor industry magazines so that they can put a current value on used and part-exchange vehicles that are brought in.

## Top Five

The company that Nick works for only sells cars made by one manufacturer. Nick's favourite makes are:

1. Vauxhall
2. Lotus
3. Porsche
4. Ferrari
5. BMW

Nick has popped over to the sales showroom to test-drive a new car. He plans to replace his old car soon.

# Pros and Cons

N ick always wanted to be a mechanic. He knew he needed qualifications, but didn't think college would suit him. As an apprentice, he can earn a wage and train at the same time. He gets all the staff perks, including paid holidays and discounts on cars or parts.

## Key Choices

Apprentices in the motor industry choose which sort of work to specialise in. The choices are:

- **Mechanical**
- **Maintenance**
- **Car Sales**
- **Electronics**
- **Customer Service**

Nick *clocks on* at 8 a.m. and works until 5 p.m. He gets an hour off for lunch, plus a morning and afternoon break.

N̶ick doesn't really see a down-side to his job. Mechanics do not earn a high wage, but it is not that low either. There are not many opportunities for promotion, but Nick doesn't think that matters if you enjoy what you do.

Accidents sometimes happen, however careful people are. There is always a first-aider on site and a well-stocked first-aid box.

For noisy, dangerous jobs such as grinding metal, Nick wears ear protectors and goggles to stop sparks flying into his eyes.

With so many tools and machines being used, the job can sometimes be dangerous. However, most of the dangers arise when people do not follow all the Health and Safety guidelines, and Bill has explained these to Nick. Nick knows that he must wear ear protectors and goggles for certain types of work, for example.

# Finding a Job

The only qualifications for being an apprentice mechanic are that, like Nick, you have a knack for fixing things. Sometimes a company will require two GCSE passes, but the main training will be on the job.

Companies are looking for someone who will repay the time and money they spend on the training. You need to show that you are keen to learn, energetic and responsible.

Nick was really pleased when he got his own bay. It showed that the company could see him staying for a long time.

Malcolm is in charge of all the workshop staff. He checks that Nick is getting all the help he needs from his mentor, Bill.

At his interview, Nick talked about the motorbike he was restoring. This showed Malcolm that Nick was passionate about engines. It also helped that Nick had worked at a petrol station on Saturdays. It showed that he liked being around cars, and that he was reliable enough to hold down a job.

# Job Know-How

### What qualifications do I need?

It depends on the company. The place where Nick works expects its apprentices to have GCSE passes in English and Mathematics at least. Apprenticeship places are limited to people aged 16 to 25, but most go to those aged 16 to 18.

### What personal qualities do I need?

Good at problem-solving, interested in cars and able to understand how machines work, keen, sociable, responsible.

### How do I apply?

Approach a local garage directly, or look in the local press for job adverts.

### Will there be an interview?

Yes – to check that you are responsible. Companies have to invest a lot of time and money training an apprentice, so they will want to be sure you will repay their confidence by working hard.

▲ **Nick sometimes has to use the company computers. Here, he is finding out about a brake pipe.**

Many schools organise **work experience** at a garage, or you could try to get a Saturday job in one. Mostly, you will be expected to clean the cars, but at least you'll get to see how everything works.

# Glossary

| | |
|---|---|
| **Allocate** | Share out. |
| **Apprentice** | Someone working towards qualifications for a job, by learning the skills in a real work place. |
| **Blowtorch** | A lamp that produces a jet of burning-hot flame. |
| **Buffed** | Rubbed to make shiny; polished. |
| **Career** | Someone's profession or job. |
| **Clock on** | To record when you arrive at work, by passing a card through a machine that has a clock inside it. When you stop work, you clock off. |
| **Conference room** | A place where meetings can be held. |
| **Courtesy car** | A car that is given to a customer to drive while their own car is at the garage. |
| **Disposable** | Throw-away. |
| **Estimate** | Make a good guess at something. |
| **Foreman** | The supervisor, who watches over the workers. |
| **Grille** | Metal grating on the front of a car. |
| **Ignite** | Catch fire, spark. |
| **Make** | The name of a company that has made a car, such as Vauxhall. |
| **Manual** | An instruction book. |
| **Mentor** | The person who acts as a leader and trainer to an apprentice. |
| **Model** | A particular type of car, such as an Astra. |
| **Panel beating** | Knocking metal sheets back into shape. |
| **Pliable** | Easily bent or moulded into shape. |
| **Qualifications** | Official requirements for a particular job. |
| **Rollcage** | A metal cage on wheels, with sides but no top, used for moving stacks of boxes. |
| **Shell** | The metal or fibre-glass body of a car. |
| **Specialist** | For a particular purpose. |
| **Spraygun** | A device used to spray paint. |
| **Upholstery** | Soft furnishings. |
| **Welding** | Using heat to join together two pieces of metal. |
| **Work experience** | An unpaid period of work, often for a week, so that a person can see what a job is like at first-hand. |

# Find Out More

This is the garage where Nick works:

**F.G. Barnes**
**Sutton Road**
**Parkwood**
**Maidstone**
**Kent ME15 9IF**

Visit the company's website, too, to find out about other branches:

**www.fgbarnes.co.uk**

Visit the Motor Industry Training Council's website:

**http://mitc.co.uk**

Find out more about further qualifications by visiting the NVQ website:

**www.dfee.gov.uk/nvq**

Find out more about starting a modern apprenticeship in the motor industry:

**www.motor-careers.co.uk/ quals/quals-school-leaver.htm**

There are lots of magazines for people interested in cars. Look in your local newsagent for:

**BBC Top Gear Magazine (www.topgear.beeb.com)**
**Car Mechanics**
**Cars & Car Conversions Magazine**

In Australia and New Zealand you can check out:

**www.newapprentices.gov.au**
**www.autocareers.com.au**

Ask at local polytechnics for apprenticeship courses.

Also, why don't you...

• Visit your local library and check out the careers section.

• Find out if there is a teacher at your school who is an expert careers advisor.

• Look in your local business directory under 'Garages' to find out who to contact for work experience placements.

# Index